CAROL M. HIGHSMITH AND TED LANDPHAIR

BOSTON

A PHOTOGRAPHIC TOUR

CRESCENT BOOKS

NEW YORK

THE AUTHORS GRATEFULLY ACKNOWLEDGE
THE SERVICES, ACCOMMODATIONS, AND SUPPORT PROVIDED BY
HILTON HOTELS CORPORATION
AND
THE COLONIAL HILTON AND RESORT
WAKEFIELD, MASSACHUSETTS
IN CONNECTION WITH THE COMPLETION OF THIS BOOK.

———

Thomas Ball, a native of nearby Charlestown, executed the equestrian statue of George Washington (page 1) in the Boston Public Garden in 1869. Ball was determined to depict Washington's steed as accurately as he portrayed the general; he visited several local stables and hired a famous local horse as his model. At dusk, the Boston Common (pages 2–3)—the nation's oldest public park, covering fifty acres—provides a muted foreground for the city's downtown skyline. The capital of Massachusetts is not a city of notable skyscrapers; it has retained its human scale and prides itself on remaining a "walking city."

This 1997 edition is published by Crescent Books, a division of Random House Value Publishing, Inc., 201 East 50th Street, New York, N.Y. 10022.

Crescent Books and colophon are trademarks of Random House Value Publishing, Inc.

Random House
New York • Toronto • London • Sydney • Auckland
http://www.randomhouse.com/

Printed and bound in China

Library of Congress Cataloging-in-Publication Data
Highsmith, Carol M., 1946–
Boston / Carol M. Highsmith and Ted Landphair.
p. cm. — (A photographic tour)
ISBN 0-517-18329-3 (hc: alk. paper)
1. Boston (Mass.)—Tours. 2. Boston (Mass.)—
Pictorial works. I. Landphair, Ted, 1942– . II. Title.
III. Series: Highsmith, Carol M., 1946– Photographic tour.
F73.18.H54 1997   96-43085
917.44´610443—dc20   CIP

8 7 6 5 4 3 2 1

———

Designed by Robert L. Wiser, Archetype Press, Inc., Washington, D.C.

All photographs by Carol M. Highsmith unless otherwise credited: map by XNR Productions, page 5; painting by Frederick Childe Hassam, gift of Miss Maud E. Appleton (courtesy, Museum of Fine Arts, Boston), page 6; Boston Public Library, page 8–21

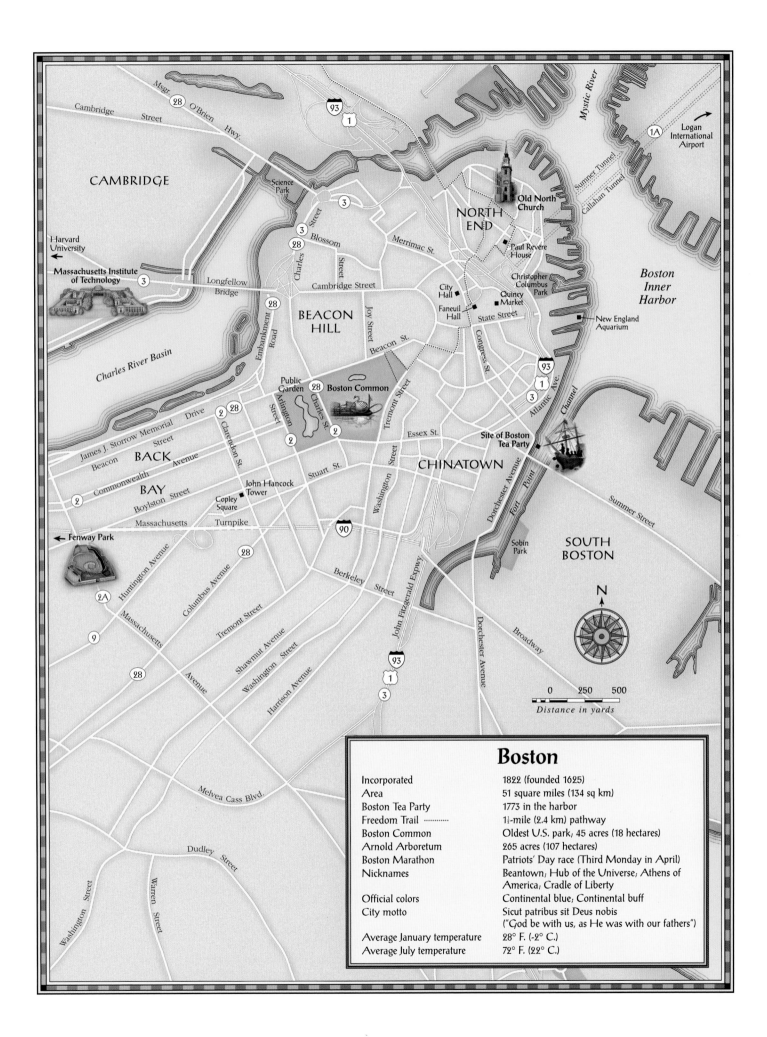

CAMBRIDGE

Msgr. O'Brien Hwy.

Cambridge Street

Harvard University →

Massachusetts Institute of Technology

Science Park

Blossom Street

Charles Street

Merrimac St.

NORTH END

Old North Church

Paul Revere House

Christopher Columbus Park

Boston Inner Harbor

Logan International Airport

Summer Tunnel

Callahan Tunnel

Mystic River

Longfellow Bridge

Cambridge Street

City Hall

Quincy Market

Faneuil Hall

State Street

New England Aquarium

BEACON HILL

Joy Street

Beacon St.

Congress St.

Charles River Basin

Embankment Road

Public Garden

Boston Common

Charles St.

Tremont Street

Arlington Street

James J. Storrow Memorial Drive

Beacon Street

Clarendon St.

Commonwealth Avenue

BACK BAY

Boylston Street

Stuart St.

Essex St.

Washington Street

CHINATOWN

Site of Boston Tea Party

Channel

Atlantic Ave.

Dorchester Avenue

Fort Point

John Hancock Tower

Copley Square

Massachusetts Turnpike

← Fenway Park

Huntington Avenue

Columbus Avenue

Tremont Street

Massachusetts Avenue

Shawmut Avenue

Washington Street

Harrison Avenue

Berkeley Street

John Fitzgerald Espwy.

Sobin Park

SOUTH BOSTON

Summer Street

Broadway

Dorchester Avenue

N

Melvea Cass Blvd.

Dudley Street

Washington Street

Warren Street

0   250   500

Distance in yards

Boston

Incorporated	1822 (founded 1625)
Area	51 square miles (134 sq km)
Boston Tea Party	1773 in the harbor
Freedom Trail ··········	1½-mile (2.4 km) pathway
Boston Common	Oldest U.S. park, 45 acres (18 hectares)
Arnold Arboretum	265 acres (107 hectares)
Boston Marathon	Patriots' Day race (Third Monday in April)
Nicknames	Beantown; Hub of the Universe; Athens of America; Cradle of Liberty
Official colors	Continental blue; Continental buff
City motto	Sicut patribus sit Deus nobis ("God be with us, as He was with our fathers")
Average January temperature	28° F. (-2° C.)
Average July temperature	72° F. (22° C.)

I F FREEDOM WERE A CONCRETE THING, SOMETHING THAT COULD BE SEEN and touched, Boston would be the place to do the seeing and touching. The Cradle of American Liberty is an endlessly fascinating living-history museum of the seventeenth and eighteenth centuries. If that were all that Boston is, it would still be well worth visiting. But it is so much more. It is a world city whose libraries, colleges, medical centers, museums and parks, and architecture compare with the best on the globe.

Boston is the nation's preeminent walking city, built to a human scale that has been preserved. So many roads and streets follow the routes of old cow paths—or permit one-way traffic only—that only a longtime Bostonian can decipher exactly where they lead. Locals say that what sometimes seems like their superior Brahmin bearing stems not from their pedigrees or intellectual accomplishments, but from the simple fact that they know the town's shortcuts. Superhighways skirt the city, save for one that cuts right across Frederick Law Olmsted's "Emerald Necklace" of serene parks and greenswards on its way across the Charles River. Approval of that concrete intrusion into the lovely Back Bay neighborhood—and the decision to raze another old community of homes in the West End in the name of urban renewal—are seen as so misguided today that historic buildings and green spaces are doubly and triply protected.

None more so than the sixteen sites on the Freedom Trail, a self-guided walking tour of fifteen Revolutionary War and other colonial sites conveniently marked with red bricks or a red line down the sidewalk. National Park Service ranger tours, commencing from a visitor center at 15 State Street, cover six of the locations: the Old South Meeting House, the Boston Massacre site, Paul Revere's house, the Old North Church, and the Old State House—the British "royal offices" prior to the revolution—and Faneuil Hall, the town market and meeting hall where the flames of revolution were first ignited. Costumed "sailors" (and a few damsels) assist in interpretation at the USS *Constitution* across the mouth of the Charles in Charlestown Yard; so impregnable to cannonballs had the ship's tough copper sheathing and live-oak hull seemed to British adversaries in the War of 1812 that one of the *Constitution*'s sailors dubbed her "Old Ironsides." (The Freedom Trail's red line, naturally, does not extend across the Charles to the warship.) Visitors are on their own at Trail sites like the Benjamin Franklin statue, the Bunker Hill Monument, and the Granary Burial Ground, where John Hancock, Paul Revere, Sam Adams, and the victims of the Boston Massacre are interred.

Other stops include the King's Chapel, which was the nation's first Unitarian church; the Old Corner Bookstore, a favorite of Ralph Waldo Emerson and Nathaniel Hawthorne; and the 1795 Massachusetts State House and Archives Museum, designed by Charles Bulfinch. Its gilded dome glimmers through the oaks of the Common and can be seen for miles upriver.

Visitors are advised to bring sturdy shoes to Boston, as there is yet another fascinating historical walking path to be trod: the Black Heritage Trail on the North Slope of Beacon Hill. Beginning on little Smith Court, where African Americans once occupied all of the houses, it passes Boston's first interracial school, a house that was a stop on southern slaves' Underground Railway to freedom, and a plaque honoring the 54th Massachusetts Volunteer Infantry—the Union Army's first black regiment. Open to visitors is the African Meeting House, the oldest black church in the nation that is still standing. The structure, known early in its history as the "Black Faneuil Hall," served as a church, school, meetinghouse, and nexus of the anti-slavery crusade. Abolitionists William Lloyd Garrison, Frederick Douglass, Sojourner Truth, and Charles Sumner all declaimed from its pulpit. Restoration of the structure, begun in 1986 and supported by a $1.1-million National Park Service grant—included the re-installation of the

The Boston Museum of Fine Arts owns the shimmering Boston Common at Twilight, *a gift of Maud E. Appleton. Frederick Chide Hassam's oil on canvas was created in 1885–6.*

Mount Vernon Street on Beacon Hill was a winter wonderland on this winter day in 1923. Most everyone wisely stayed inside and certainly did not attempt to drive up the hill.

entire balcony, which had been disassembled and put in storage following a 1973 fire. Ironically, the thrall of segregation was once so strong, even in liberal Boston, that at the original dedication in 1854 free blacks were forced to sit in that balcony in their own church while whites occupied the premium pews below.

The story of Boston as a settled place begins with John Winthrop and his band of about 750 pious Puritans who sailed in eleven ships from wicked England in 1630 with a charter from King James I in hand, seeking a "City Upon a Hill." The charter entitled their "Massachusetts Bay Company" to occupy a sliver of land near the mouth of the Charles River and reaching, at least in theory, as far west as land extended. Other English religious dissidents called Pilgrims had preceded the Puritans to New England, founding a settlement in Plimoth, south of Boston, and other Puritans were already in place to the north in Naumkeag (later called Salem). Upon landing, Winthrop and his people spread out, forming separate settlements that would later become towns like Medford, Dorchester, Saugus . . . and Boston. Winthrop himself and about 150 others accepted the invitation of the lone white settler they encountered at the mouth of the Charles, Anglican cleric William Blackstone, and took up residence in a settlement they called "Boston" after a town back home in Lincolnshire. It was a crude place, built among the marshes along Spring Lane in what would one day be called Boston's North End. Unaccustomed to company, the Reverend Blackstone soon left for Rhode Island, but the Puritans named a road after him. So full of swamps and brambles was the neighborhood that early Bostonians derisively referred to it as "the Island of North Boston." Houses were scattered in no apparent order on hillsides and in dales, so that streets wound to and fro rather than in any logical pattern. And it is thus today in many parts of town.

Boston's Puritans were initially guided by the Reverend John Cotton at the First Church. The Second Church of Boston—known today as the Old North Church—was founded in the North End in 1650. The Second Church was led by one Increase Mather, who would become an early Harvard graduate and patriarch of a Boston dynasty. Increase Mather was joined in the leadership of the church by his son, Cotton, a prolific chronicler who dabbled in witch-hunting when he was not writing. His most famous work, *Magnalia Christi Americana*, traced the history of the Puritans and their churches in the New World. So accomplished would Cotton Mather become as an astronomer, botanist, and student of physics that he would be elected to the British Royal Society in 1713.

Boston's first markets and wharves were located on the North End, ensuring that its most prosperous citizens would take up residence there. The Puritans had expected to farm in the New World, but they soon realized that the sea held out their best chances for wealth. By the late 1600s Boston merchants were sending cod to England, importing manufactured goods, and distilling rum, which they traded for West Indian sugar and slaves. Somehow this was all reconciled with their holier-than-thou religious beliefs. Until the colony grew too large to be kept under the church's thumb, dissension from stern Puritan teachings was not tolerated. Free spirits like Roger Williams or Anne Hutchinson who argued for religious tolerance were banished, as were Quakers and members of other faiths. Those who persisted in questioning the church's conventions, like Mary Dyer, were hanged.

But eventually the Puritans caved in. Cotton Mather himself opened communion to Baptists and Lutherans, among others; Methodists and Anglicans built their own churches in the North End; and people of many political leanings moved into the neighborhood. Colonel Thomas Hutchinson, a prickly aristocrat who would later become the detested royal governor, lived in the North End. So did populist Paul Revere, a goldsmith, silversmith, and engraver who resented the colonists' second-class citizenship and would later be an enthusiastic participant in the Boston Tea Party.

Antagonism toward Britain had begun with the return of the monarchs of the House of Stuart, beginning in 1660. Earlier in the century, the Stuarts had been too busy dealing with General Oliver Cromwell and his revolutionaries to pay much attention to Massachusetts Bay and the other colonies. Charles I literally lost his head in all the fulmination, and then Cromwell and his son ruled as "lord protectors" for eleven years. But thereafter, when Charles II took the throne, he initiated tightfisted rule of the colonies, imposing new taxes and the hated Navigation Acts that required the colonies to trade exclusively with Mother England. When merchants ignored these acts, Charles revoked royal colonial charters and placed all of New England under one administration. Its first governor-general, Sir Edmund Andros, got off on the wrong foot with Puritan Boston by converting the Old South Meeting House into an Anglican church and demanding property-tax payments from wealthy landowners. Monarchs William III and

The shadow of the Custom House tower falls on snow-covered rooftops downtown in January 1936. As usual in pragmatic Boston, traffic seems to be getting through just fine.

Mary II decreed that all landowning males would have a vote in colonial affairs. This reduced forever the sway of the Puritan clergy. The merchant class, Peter Faneuil and Thomas Hancock—John's uncle—among them, grew wealthier, despite their tax burden. They built mansions on Beacon Hill and ruled the city informally but benevolently; Faneuil, for instance, built the city's famous public hall and marketplace with his own funds.

While some Bostonians prospered in the "triangle trade" of fish, molasses, finished British goods, and slaves, others suffered and chafed under British rule. When George III imposed several new taxes, including the 1765 Stamp Act levy on legal documents, many in Boston simply refused to pay. A committee of firebrands who called themselves the "Sons of Liberty"—including Paul Revere and John Hancock—led street protests and a boycott of British goods. King George lifted the Stamp Act but imposed new tariffs on goods like paper and tea. Mobs spilled from homes and taverns to protest, and in the "Boston Massacre" of March 5, 1770, five colonists were killed and several others wounded. Three years later, Revere and a few dozen other Sons of Liberty, poorly disguised as Indians, took out their wrath against the tea tax by dumping a cargo of British tea into Boston Harbor. This Boston Tea Party only steeled the Crown's resolve to assert control. Parliament ordered the harbor closed and installed a military governor, Sir Thomas Gage. In Massachusetts and elsewhere, talk of revolution spread. In September 1774, the First Continental Congress, meeting in Philadelphia, authorized the recruitment of a colonial army.

Back on Boston's North End, Paul Revere organized "watchers" to keep an eye on the British, and he rode to warn the colonists that British forces were coming by sea in April 1775 to search out and seize a suspected cache of colonial weapons in Concord. With considerable help from poet Henry Wadsworth Longfellow ("Listen, my children, and you shall hear/Of the midnight ride of Paul Revere"), Revere's place in American history was thus assured. The colonists might have guessed that the British would advance on Lexington by sea and thence up the Charles because a land advance would have been foolhardy. Boston, in those pre-landfill days, was only one-third its current size. There were no convenient bridges to Cambridge across which to begin an advance on the colonists' inland positions. Boston was ringed by a quagmire of bogs—the "fens" that would one day be freshened and beautifully landscaped. Lieutenant Colonel Francis Smith, placed in command of the expedition by General Gage, would have had to march his men and cannons south to Roxbury, then north around the swamps to Harvard Square. Instead he opted for the boat ride to Cambridge and a much shorter march to Concord.

Little did the British know that eighteenth-century guerrilla warfare awaited them. On the Lexington Battle Green (Common), the British were met with the first skirmish from colonial "Minute Men," eight of whom died in the fighting. Down the road, the Redcoats themselves tasted blood, death, and defeat for the first time at Concord's North Bridge. There, the "shot heard 'round the world" signaled the start of a revolutionary war from which there would be no turning back. More than seventy Redcoats died at Concord and in their retreat back to Boston. In June 1775, in a battle the British won, another thirteen hundred of their soldiers would be killed or wounded at Bunker Hill. Soon afterward, George Washington arrived in Cambridge and

There was little mechanization in Boston's Market District early in the century. Wagons brought in the produce and meat, and pushcarts displayed the goods and carried them throughout town.

took command of colonial forces. He plotted strategy while the British laid siege to Boston through the bitter winter. In March 1776, Washington directed a skillful bombardment of British ships in Boston Harbor, forcing thousands of Redcoat soldiers and their Tory supporters to flee Boston for good. From that point until independence was achieved seven years later, Boston was spared further fighting. (Two centuries later a Bostonian would remark over coffee that had the British realized what riches the vast continent would later reveal, they might have fought harder and longer, bringing in whatever reinforcements were necessary to hold on to the rebellious colonies.)

After the Revolution, control of Boston fell to a new aristocratic class of merchants and artisans who built mansions on Beacon Hill and striking new public buildings downtown. Charles Bulfinch, for example, spruced up Faneuil Hall, joined the "Mount Vernon Proprietors" in carving out Beacon Hill townhouse developments, and created a magnificent new gilded-dome Massachusetts statehouse before moving to Washington to work on the U.S. Capitol. The members of this new gentry were soon dubbed, derogatorily, "Brahmins," as if they were a snooty, impenetrable upper caste. Some Brahmin families traced their heritage to the *Mayflower* or to John Winthrop's ship, the *Arabella*, or claimed to. Bluebloods would keep political control of the city until 1884, when Hugh O'Brien, the first of a long line of Irish mayors, took office.

Leslie Jones was a prolific photographer who captured Boston from many angles in the first four decades of the twentieth century. This is Faneuil Hall, seen from the Ames Building in 1936.

Meantime, as more colleges appeared, Boston became America's undisputed intellectual capital and, at least to some in the North, its conscience as well. The abolitionist movement, fanned by editor William Lloyd Garrison, took form in Boston; so did the first stirrings of the crusade for women's rights, led by Bostonians Margaret Fuller and Lydia Maria Child.

They changed the nation, but it was Irish politicians who changed Boston. Poor Irish Catholics had arrived by the tens of thousands in the middle 1800s. Most lived in slums in South Boston and, if they were lucky, found menial jobs as ditchdiggers on canals and railways. At almost every turn, they were greeted with loathing and violence. Signs reading ONLY PROTESTANTS NEED APPLY FOR JOBS abounded. Mobs attacked Irish settlements and even burned down a convent, and priests were denied permission to enter the city's charity hospitals to administer last rites to the dying. For the Irish, neighborhood politics and service as police and firefighters were the only road out of poverty and into power.

South Boston was the city's largest Irish enclave. Who could forget "The Singing Mayor"— John F. "Honey Fitz" Fitzgerald, who would croon "Sweet Adeline" with little provocation? Or the "Mayor of the Poor"—James "Boss" Curley, Boston's four-time leader who once ran for city council from his jail cell (and won), won one race for mayor while he was also a U.S. Democratic representative (and kept both jobs), and, free on bail after a federal conviction for mail fraud, immediately took a train home and organized his own parade? Ten thousand people cheered, and a brass band led the procession with its rendition of "Hail the Conquering Hero Comes." Three times after World War II, Boston Irish congressmen—Joseph W. Martin Jr., John W. McCormack, and Thomas P. "Tip" O'Neill Jr.—rose through the ranks of the House to become Speaker. Somehow, Martin managed to do it as a Republican. These men, and the

The Custom House dominated the skyline—such as it was in Boston in 1929—around Haymarket Square at a time when the streets did not seem narrow or crowded at all.

scions of Boston businessman millionaire Joseph P. Kennedy, represented a departure from the ward-heeling, cigar-chomping Irish "pols" of the past. Though he was a grandson of "Honey Fitz," Kennedy's son John Fitzgerald Kennedy became the first of the idealistic, progressive Kennedys in politics when he was elected to the U.S. House in 1946. President Kennedy's boyhood home on Beals Street in suburban Brookline is now a National Historic Site. The John F. Kennedy Memorial Library in South Boston, the repository of the martyred president's papers and many of his belongings, offers an unobstructed view of the ocean that both JFK and his brother Robert loved.

As Boston politics evolved, so did its landscape. An estuary known as the "Muddy River," off Boston's Back Bay, was an open sewer for 150 years. But it and its surrounding fens changed for the better once Frederick Law Olmsted, the nation's first great landscape architect, moved his offices from New York to the Boston suburb of Brookline in 1883. Olmsted and his partner, Calvert Vaux, had designed New York's Central Park. Appointed Boston's park commissioner, he wasted little time reshaping Boston's topography to solve drainage problems and create

Boston's Italian fishermen worked nearly every day that ice did not cover the harbor—but not this Easter Sunday in 1930. That was a solemn family holiday for most of Catholic Boston.

"public pleasure gardens." The result was the Emerald Necklace. Three old and delightful parks—the Boston Common, the adjacent Public Garden, and the long Commonwealth Avenue Mall—were already in place (though never so pruned and pretty as when Olmsted supervised them). The pentagonal Boston Common, America's oldest public park, had been used as a training ground by both British and colonial soldiers, and sheep and cows drank from its frog pond. The nation's first subterranean streetcar—soon called a "subway"—opened underneath the Common in 1897. Bostonians once clammed and fished in the estuary of the Charles River where the twenty-four-acre Public Garden now draws throngs of visitors. It was ruled forever public in an 1859 ordinance. Replete with fountains, flower beds, and statues—including Thomas Ball's 1869 equestrian statue of George Washington and a statue dedicated to a medical miracle, the development of ether—the Public Garden is best loved for its twenty-passenger swan boats that ply its lagoon at a languorous two miles an hour. The boats were inspired by the Wagner opera *Lohengrin.* "Comm Av," as most everyone in Boston calls Commonwealth Avenue, was deliberately designed as a long and straight Victorian boulevard through the Back Bay, as an antidote to the spaghetti-bowl tangle of streets elsewhere in town. Its one-hundred-foot-wide central mall is graced with flowering magnolias, heroic and whimsical statues, and plenty of park benches.

Olmsted tied the Common, Public Garden, and Comm Av to a string of other rustic parks farther to the west. They included a series of bridges and lush plantings in the stagnant Fens. Later, community gardens, landscape architect Arthur Shurtleff's formal rose garden outside the Museum of Fine Arts, and several war memorials further opened the Fens to public enjoyment. Olmsted turned remnants of the Muddy River into a man-made riverway, a linear ribbon of green connecting to Jamaica Pond and another park that would bear his name. Next in the Necklace came the Arnold Arboretum, a 265-acre "botanical and horticultural museum without walls." Its hills, valleys, woods, ponds, and streams harbor the Northern Hemisphere's premier collection of hardy trees, shrubs, and vines. The final jewel is Franklin Park, home of the city's first-rate zoo.

Boston is America's city of firsts. It was the nation's first commercial center, first significant

port, the seed ground of the Revolution. It was the first center of learning, the first place where immigrants in large numbers debarked. Why, then, did New York and Philadelphia—and later, upstart inland cities like Chicago—become the megalopolises, and not Boston? Unfavorable geography, in the form of those fens, hemmed the city in. Bitter winters and Boston's distance from the heartland discouraged the development of good roads. Though it built its airport a stone's throw from downtown, Boston never had the land to create a giant air hub.

But the answer also lies in the Boston mind-set, its love of things old and tested and suspicion of too much change. Boston relishes its role as the trustee of a good portion of America's colonial heritage, and it approaches modernity with caution. Even visitors take comfort in knowing that they can leave Boston, perhaps for twenty years or more, and return to find most of the places they love still intact. Boston remains difficult to reach and tricky to get around in, and the natives seem to prefer it that way. There's a part of the Bostonian's stoic character—adopted by newcomers almost immediately after they move in—that it does a person good to feel a little discomfort: don't let a little thing like a traffic jam or a nor'east blizzard slow you down. Lace up your boots and get on with it. Besides, September to April is the glorious theater, ballet, and indoor festival season—food for the heart and mind.

But there's an ironic twist. At the same time that Boston remains enraptured by its past, it has also been the center of remarkable intellectual innovation, owing in no small measure to Greater Boston's sixty or so exceptional colleges. Computer and biomedical miracles begin here. As a result, Boston is one of the nation's three top venture-capital cities, and a number of people

working in Financial District skyscrapers are engaged in little more than finding and bankrolling the next genius researcher or start-up company. Of the *Boston Globe*'s top twenty-five on its list of one hundred publicly held companies in 1996, four, including No. 1 Teradyne Inc., were electronics companies; seven produced computer software, circuit boards, or other computer products or provided Internet services; and three specialized in communications equipment. Information Age products had replaced heavy industry as the backbone of Boston's economy. Regrettably for the workforce, once those companies flower and it comes time to build the new creations, operations tend to move elsewhere, where tax, land, and labor costs are lower. Once the elsewhere was south, in Tennessee and the Carolinas, or west, especially California. Now the brainchildren of Boston's inventors and innovators are as likely to be built in a shops abroad, reflecting, again, Boston's global destiny. The vagaries of innovation produced boom and bust cycles and led to a gradual loss of population. The 1950 federal census counted more than eight hundred thousand people inside city limits. In 1990, the count was down to fewer than six hundred thousand. Yet Boston managed to get wealthier all the while, as newcomers of means moved in and refurbished whole neighborhoods, notably in the Fenway and the South End.

Bostonians seem to the enjoy the company of a quarter-million college students from around the nation and the world. The oldest college of all, Harvard University in Cambridge, was created as a training ground for Puritan ministers in 1638 so the colonists' sons would not have to return to Europe to study. In 1865 Harvard gained freedom from church control and

A swan boat in Boston's Public Garden got a most fitting complement of passengers— a group of Navy Waves—on a summer's day in 1932.

gradually developed into the prototype of the modern university, with professional and graduate schools complementing its rigorous liberal-arts foundation. It would be a century plus ten years more, however, before Harvard admitted women by fully integrating Radcliffe College—with whom Harvard students had been sharing classes for years. Today Harvard Yard—and a newsstand outside the campus gate that brings in publications from around the globe—have become tourist attractions.

The constellation of universities and their faculty members and students has helped cement Boston's reputation as a liberal enclave in conservative New England. Outside the city, one still hears Harvard, for instance, referred to as "The People's Republic of Cambridge," and outlanders have not forgotten students' part in casting Massachusetts for George McGovern in 1972, when only the votes of Massachusetts, the District of Columbia, and some U.S. territories kept Richard Nixon from the first Electoral College sweep since Ulysses S. Grant shut out Horace Greeley exactly a century earlier. William Cowper Brann, who published a newspaper in Texas called *The Iconoclast*, observed in the 1890s that "Boston runs to brains as well as to beans and brown bread. But she is cursed with an army of cranks whom nothing short of a straitjacket or a swamp elm club will ever control." Bostonians see their liberal reputation another way: they say it upholds the determination of colonial leaders to make the nation a place of free and open debate, where everyone's opinion carries equal weight.

If Boston ever did "run to beans," as Brann maintained, "Beantown" does not seem to serve many beans any longer. While there are still "Beanpot Classic" sporting tournaments, and hundreds of restaurants serving "scrod" (likely a cod or haddock, but just as often an unidentifiable "catch of the day"), except in Bostonians' homes the visitor will be hard-pressed to find a bowl of classic dark, slow-baked, steeped-in-molasses beans. One of the videos shown to visitors at the Prudential Tower Skywalk does disclose a "secret recipe for Boston Baked Beans" (truly beans with a view). And there's a popular sports bar called the Bean Pot. But that's about the extent of the remaining influence of beans—save for the coffee bean, which has a tight grip on the town. Thanks again, in part, to the college influence, every other corner seems to support a coffee bar.

James Michael Curley dominated Boston politics—as mayor, Massachusetts governor, and U.S. congressman—from 1920 until 1950. In 1949 he accepted the support of a four-legged friend, "Thor."

Boston was long regarded as a culinary backwater until well into the 1990s. Since the city eschewed trendiness in fashion and music, it followed that its restaurants would be dependable but unspectacular, their clientele frugal and relatively undiscriminating. The picture began to change, however, when the U.S. Bureau of Labor Statistics revealed in 1993 that Boston, the nation's twentieth-largest city, was tied for sixth in per-capita spending on food away from home. Then, in 1996, two Boston chefs—Michael Schlow of Cafe Louis and Barbara Lynch at Galleria Italiana—made *Food & Wine* magazine's coveted list of the ten top new chefs in America, and heads began to turn.

Thanks in no small measure to the *Cheers* television show, which played for eleven top-rated seasons, plus reruns, Beacon Hill is Boston's best-known neighborhood. Its well-kept buildings and impeccably presented residents—with their faintly British accents, gray and tweed suits, and red-silk ties and ascots—are certainly stereotypical of the Hill's Brahmin past. Not so well known are the warrens of students and young working people on Beacon Hill who can afford the rent, or the vibrant nightlife on Charles, the Hill's one commercial street.

A neophyte campaigner—John F. Kennedy, running for Congress—joins two veterans, Mayor James Curley (left) and Governor Maurice Tobin—at a Veterans of Foreign Wars convention in 1946.

In contrast to staid Beacon Hill, the South End, Chinatown, and Allston are dynamic neighborhoods. Thousands of students have found space in triple-deck homes in Allston, where the noise level is high and the automobile inventory runs from luxury cars to barely ambulatory wrecks. The South End, arguably the nation's largest Victorian neighborhood next to Brooklyn's Park Slope, had festered into a slum but has been rejuvenated by couples and young families of a dozen ethnic extractions who have rehabilitated hundreds of "bowfront" brownstone row houses; on a bowfront, half of the front façade is rounded like a bay window that extends the full three or four stories of the building's height. Both Allston and South End are laced with eclectic shops and restaurants as well. And Boston's small but rapidly expanding Chinatown has subsumed and cleaned up a dreadful neighborhood of brothels and flophouses that Bostonians called the "Combat Zone."

Photographers searching for a neatly packaged skyline shot of the city will be frustrated. Its tall buildings pop up in widely separated clumps, first downtown, in and around the Financial District, then on Beacon Hill (these are not really tall, but the hill gives them elevation). And the city's two loftiest structures, the Prudential Tower and the John Hancock Building, loom off by themselves, a mile away from downtown on Boylston Street between the Back Bay and South End. Prudential Center, sometimes shortened locally to "the Pru," was built in the 1960s on the site of an old railroad yard. It features a shopping mall, a direct connection to the city's spacious convention center, and its skyscraping office tower, whose fiftieth-floor Skywalk offers a panoramic view of the city, Cambridge, and even (on a clear day) the beginnings of far-off New Hampshire. It is also an excellent vantage point from which to see Boston's other signature skyscraper—and New England's tallest building—designer I. M. Pei's 790-foot John

The Boston Bruins' Willie O'Ree was the first black player in the National Hockey League at a time when the league had only six teams and outstanding players at every position.

Hancock Tower, which was finished in 1976. This tower, which has its own popular observatory ten stories higher than the Pru's, experienced incredible setbacks in its early years, as several of its panes of glass shattered and fell to the rooftops and ground below. At one point, Hancock employees with binoculars were assigned to keep watch on the building twenty-four hours a day, looking for telltale signs that a window was about to disintegrate. Eventually every one of the thousands of panes—more than thirteen acres of glass all told—was replaced, and the problem disappeared.

Reflecting in the Hancock Tower's glass are the buildings of historic Copley Square, including the sophisticated Copley Place mall, built in the early 1980s; old Trinity Church; and the magnificent Boston Public Library. The 1877 Trinity Church was architect Henry Hobson Richardson's Romanesque masterwork. Not only did he design a breathtaking building outside and engage the day's greatest artists—including John La Farge and William Morris—to execute astounding interior paintings and stained glass, but he also created an engineering marvel. The massive church rests on squishy Back Bay soil, far above bedrock. Richardson solved the problem by driving more than forty-five hundred wooden pilings deep into the ooze. McKim, Mead & White's Boston Public Library Building, which opened in 1895, is entered through massive bronze doors designed by Daniel Chester French, who would later sculpt the statue for the Lincoln Memorial in Washington. Like Richardson across the square, Charles McKim engaged top artists of the day to ornament the library's interior. Edward Abbey, for one, interpreted the legend of the Holy Grail, and John Singer Sargent depicted scenes from the history of Judaism and Christianity in a series of captivating murals.

"Greater Boston" is harder to define than are the metropolitan areas of many cities. Many citizens of nearby Milton and Quincy, Peabody and Dedham, Needham and Braintree, have little to do with the big city. Conversely, some communities outside the Interstate 95 belt line around town are directly tied to Boston, or at least to its tourist economy. Buses leave regularly for Lexington, Concord, and North Shore communities like Marblehead, Salem, and Gloucester. Marblehead is a New England sailing mecca where "Race Week" in July draws competitors from throughout the East Coast. Salem, once the center of witchcraft hysteria, produced America's first millionaires among the men who financed and sailed the sea trade with the Orient. Salem is also home to an array of stunning Federal-style homes, including "The House of Seven Gables" made famous by native Nathaniel Hawthorne. Gloucester, the nation's oldest seaport, is a quintessential New England fishing village from which the fleet and whale-watching boats depart daily. To the regret of its fishermen, however, many of the catches that are unloaded on Gloucester's docks come from boats of Canadian, Icelandic, and Scandinavian registry.

Far to the south, three other destinations—Cape Cod, Martha's Vineyard, and Nantucket—are linked to the Boston way of life. Cape Cod, the scorpion-shaped peninsula of Massachusetts, has been a favorite weekend and vacation getaway for well over a century. Its ring of beaches—including the thirty-mile stretch of pristine dunes and beaches at Cape Cod National Seashore—is unmatched in New England. So are Cape Cod's distinctive cottages, whose comfy style was later copied across the nation. Lawns on the Cape are sometimes tiny but often festooned with flowers. The charming towns on Cape Cod offer superb antique shops, art galleries, restful bed-and-breakfast inns, and family-style seafood restaurants—with an emphasis on lobster. There's a John F. Kennedy Memorial in Hyannis, but don't expect to get a glimpse of the shrouded Kennedy family compound in nearby Hyannisport. And don't, if you have any choice, attempt to cross the Sagamore Bridge onto the peninsula on a summer Friday afternoon. Half of Boston, or so it seems, will have the same idea, and the backup will serve as a foul prelude to a pleasant excursion.

Martha's Vineyard and Nantucket, once glacial outwash plains, are both islands lying south of Cape Cod in Nantucket Sound. More upscale than the Cape, both are full of heaths, cliffs, biking and hiking trails, saltbox houses, and a precious commodity: peace and quiet. Triangular Martha's Vineyard was named by English explorer Bartholomew Gosnold in 1602 for his daughter back home and for the wild grapes that he found growing in profusion. "The Vineyard's" wealth is more conspicuous than in understated, old-money Nantucket, and the island became an even more noteworthy vacation destination when President Bill Clinton and his family chose it for their summer vacations. Boston newspaperman Walter Prichard Eaton, who wrote a book about New England, described Martha's Vineyard as "a land of old towns, new cottages, high cliffs, white sails, green fairways, salt water, wild fowl, and the steady pull of an ocean breeze." Nantucket, from the Indian word *Nanticut*, meaning "Far-Away Land," is a town in the midst of the sea, full of cobbled lanes and byways, open moors, and delightful shops that hark back to the days when it was a thriving whaling port.

Getaways to the islands, the Maine seashore, or the Vermont, New Hampshire, or Western Massachusetts mountains are *de rigueur* in Boston. But there is plenty to do back home.

Baseball's first superstar, Babe Ruth, played in Boston as a pitcher for the Red Sox. He is shown here, ignominiously ending his career in 1938, back in town as an over-the-hill outfielder with the Braves.

The Museum of Science, near "Mass General" Hospital, was a pioneer in "hands-on" education. It maintains more than four hundred exhibits in anthropology, medicine, astronomy (at its Hayden Planetarium) and other sciences. The Christian Scientists' "Mother Church" complex, south of Back Bay, includes the offices of the *Christian Science Monitor* and a gigantic stained-glass globe called the "Mapparium." Both the Computer Museum, whose exhibits include a "Walk-Through Computer," and the raucously enjoyable Children's Museum, are housed in an old warehouse building across the Congress Street Bridge on "Museum Wharf." So is the "Boston Tea Party Ship and Museum," where tourists are invited to join in heaving bales of tea overboard.

The Museum of Fine Arts, in a 1909 Beaux Arts building (and 1981 I. M. Pei west wing) on Huntington Avenue, boasts the world's largest collection of Asiatic art under one roof, as well as spectacular exhibits of European and American paintings, textiles and costumes, and even musical instruments. The New England Aquarium on Central Wharf features playful penguins as well as a cast of predators and other creatures from the briny deep. On the North End, Paul Revere's house, the only surviving building from seventeenth-century Boston—and an adjacent museum interpreting his life—are open to tours. In the Fenway, the Isabella Stewart Gardner Museum, built in the style of a fifteenth-century Venetian palace, overlooks an interior flowering courtyard and houses more than 2,500 art objects. And there are surprises in surrounding towns, including a museum of transportation, featuring vintage automobiles, in a mammoth carriage house in Brookline; a museum of technology at MIT in Cambridge, and a Science Center at Harvard that includes a collection of historical scientific instruments; the home of Louisa May Alcott and her family in Concord; the Kendall Whaling Museum, featur-

ing whaling artifacts and art from a dozen nations, in Sharon; a forty-five-acre landscaped flower arrangement at the "Garden in the Woods" in Framingham; and the Sports Museum of New England, in Cambridge, displaying jerseys and other paraphernalia of the region's professional and college teams.

College sports, understandably, are passionately followed in the Boston area. So are the pros, though the passions surrounding them have often been frustration and grief. Baseball's Boston Red Sox, playing at cozy Fenway Park, with its "Green Monster" left-field wall tempting home-run hitters, have broken the hearts of New England fans more often than they have rewarded their supporters. After decades of sending forth legendary champions, the Boston Celtics basketball franchise fell upon hard times in the era of multimillionaire free-agent players in the 1990s. Hockey's Bruins, who joined the Celtics in a move from the storied "Baaston Gaahden" to the new Fleet Center arena in 1995, fared better against their National Hockey League rivals. The New England Patriots, anchored in Foxboro twenty miles south of town, have vacillated between mediocrity and championship contention in their years in the American and National football leagues. Of course, the cheapest, and one of the most enjoyable, vicarious sporting diversions is hanging over the Boston University and Eliot bridges—and the John W. Weeks footbridge—over the Charles and watching sailing regattas and sculling practices and competitions.

In any season in Boston, the Red Sox and local politics are likely to dominate a conversation over coffee or lunch. Then, to prove that this is indeed America's walking city, Bostonians are apt to finish their coffee and cranberry muffins—or chowder and Italian pastries—and take a long stroll on the Common or Public Garden, as if they were discovering them for the first time.

OVERLEAF: Beacon Hill and various office buildings rise above the Charles River. Now the city's most fashionable neighborhood, "the Hill" was once an undesirable labyrinth of cow paths, bramble bushes, and pastureland. It had three definable peaks called Trimountain, but two were leveled by developers. The painter John Singleton Copley had the good fortune to own the entire south slope, which became, in time, the enclave of New England's social elite.

Andrzej P. Pitynski created the Partisans sculpture (above) on the edge of the Boston Common. Flowering shrubs (right) can be enjoyed even while strolling outside the grounds of the Public Garden adjacent to the Common. The gleaming State Capitol dome (opposite) looms over both parks. The Common is to Boston what a green is to a thousand other New England towns: a place where freemen once grazed their animals, where no buildings ever stood, and where people today find respite from the bustle of daily life. Unlike the Public Garden, it was not created by a landscape architect; its open space was taken for granted by all the town's citizens.

Self-taught architect Charles Bulfinch designed the Massachusetts State House (opposite). John Hancock owned the pastureland on which it rose from 1795 to 1797. Atop the gilded dome is a lantern capped with a pine-cone figure, symbolic of the state's extensive forestland. Paul Revere and Sons replaced the original whitewash-shingle dome with a copper one, painted gray, in 1802. It was gilded during the Civil War and briefly painted black during the security-conscious days of World War II. Thanks to additions and extensions, the statehouse is now six times its original size. Just down Beacon Street stands the King's Chapel Parish House (above), known today less for its architecture than for the purple hue of its windows. This actually resulted from a mistake—too much manganese oxide in the panes—by the English glass manufacturer. Now the windows are a tourist attraction.

Greek Revival is the architectural fashion in much of Beacon Hill's South Slope (opposite and left). When John Singleton Copley, a Tory sympathizer, fled to England after the Revolution, the Mount Vernon Properties syndicate purchased his land and built dozens of mansions and squares. While it bears no resemblance to the set of Cheers, on television, the Bull & Finch Pub on Beacon Street (above) inspired the long-running show. OVERLEAF: In the African Meeting House—known as the "Black Faneuil Hall"—on the Hill's North Slope, abolitionists railed against slavery. The building, which bears the scars of a devastating fire in 1973, is a featured stop on Boston's Black Heritage Trail.

Old City Hall (above), a complicated Second Empire structure, was the local seat of government until 1969. It is now a restaurant and office building. King's Chapel (right) was founded by the Church of England in 1686 as a place of worship for British soldiers. The present building, which replaced a small wooden structure, features four-foot-thick walls. It was designed by Newport, Rhode Island, architect Peter Harrison and begun in 1749. Because its builders ran out of funds, King's Chapel's steeple was never completed. Among the special pews inside was one where condemned prisoners could hear a sermon before they were hanged down the street on the Common.

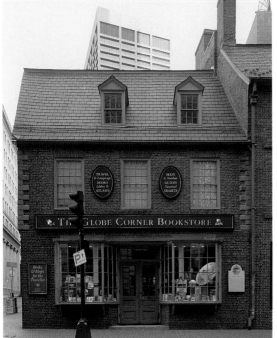

Downtown Crossing features a pedestrian mall that passes between Macy's— the historic Jordan Marsh location— and the Filene's Building (left), one of the last works of noted Chicago architect Daniel Burnham. Filene's Basement, the famous discounter, is a separate entity from the main department store upstairs. About 1718, apothecary Thomas Crease built a rose-brick house on the original site of the home of religious dissenters William and Anne Hutchinson. Crease's home eventually became the Old Corner Bookstore (above) in 1828. Upstairs, Ticknor and Fields published the works of Thoreau, Dickens, Longfellow, Hawthorne, and others. Today the building again houses a bookstore, owned by the Boston Globe.

Dozens of famous places in Boston begin with the word "Old." Here's another: the Old Granary Burial Ground (above), the last resting place of Paul Revere, John Hancock, Samuel Adams, and Elizabeth "Mother" Goose. At Boston's eerie Holocaust Memorial Park (right) near Faneuil Hall, steam rising from grates and glass towers embossed with Holocaust victims' tattoo numbers all too vividly recall the barbarism of Adolf Hitler's Nazi regime. Across the way at Quincy Market (overleaf), vendors still operate from pushcarts, and entertainment is lively and sometimes bizarre. An extension of the Faneuil Hall Marketplace, which at the time lay at the edge of Boston Harbor, Quincy Hall was named for Mayor Josiah Quincy, under whose watch the work was done. Twentieth-century renovations saved the increasingly seedy granite structure from destruction and inspired similar downtown "festival marketplace" restorations in other cities.

A street musician (above) fiddles while Boston shops at the Faneuil Hall Marketplace. The outdoor retail space (right) falls in the shadows of the hall itself. The original 1742 building on Dock Square was donated by prosperous French Huguenot merchant Peter Faneuil—which he pronounced "Funnel," according to the AIA Guide to Boston. *The structure was both an* assembly hall and English-style country market. The public exhortations of patriots like Samuel Adams and Paul Revere earned it the designation "The Cradle of Liberty," and abolitionists later declaimed there as well. It was twice rebuilt and often enlarged, all the while retaining its colonial character. Charles Bulfinch, who designed the State House on Beacon Hill, added galleries and decorative details in 1805. The building is still used for citizens' rallies and is the site for televised local and presidential primary debates.

"Ye Olde" Union Oyster House (opposite) dates to 1742, when it was Hopestill Capen's silk and dry-goods shop. In 1826 Atwood & Bacon installed the oyster bar and an open coal range and advertised itself as a fish house. The Old State House (left), Boston's oldest surviving public building, was the political center of the Massachusetts Bay Colony. Its lion and unicorn are symbols of the British Crown. Today it is a museum of Boston history. ABOVE: The 1848 Sears Block on City Hall Plaza retains Boston's most treasured sign—the 227-gallon (and two quarts, one pint, and three gills) steaming teakettle, moved from the demolished Scollay Square.

Intricate gables are repeated in the mansard roof of the Fleet Bank branch building (opposite) on Hanover Street in the city's North End. Christ, or "Old North" Church (left) on Salem Street is the city's oldest church building. The famous three-tier steeple, topped by its original weathervane, houses eight bells—the oldest in America—which a guild of Paul Revere and six friends rang as teenagers. It has never been conclusively decided whether the "two [lanterns] if by sea" signal that sent Revere on his way to warn Lexington and Concord of approaching British forces shone from this belfry or one on Second Church on North Square. British general Thomas Gage, ironically, had viewed the action at the Battle of Bunker Hill from Old North's steeple a few months earlier.

Hanover Street in front of Saint Stephen's Roman Catholic Church (opposite) is decked out for the Festival of Saint Agrippina. The 1804 church—another Charles Bulfinch creation—originally known as the New North Church, was a Congregationalist meetinghouse, then a Unitarian church, until it was sold to the Roman Catholic diocese in 1862. During the festival, churchmen carry a decorated canopy (above) into which onlookers press donations. LEFT: Salem Street's many restaurants and pizzerias have maintained the Italian flavor of the city's North End. The area, which juts out into the Atlantic Ocean, was once called the "Island of North Boston" because a canal cut it off from the city.

Sacred Heart Catholic Church (above) on North Square was originally a Protestant church with a large congregation of sea-farers and their families. Nearby on the congested square is Paul Revere's house (right), which the silversmith—and maker of false teeth—bought in 1770 when it was already almost a century old. Its over-hanging second story, called a "jetty," typifies the frame construction of the period, follow-ing the devastating fire of 1676. Revere was twice married and raised eleven children. The large family fit into this dwelling, which at the time included a third floor (since removed to restore the building to its original appearance).

ABOVE: The commander at the U.S. Naval Base at the Boston Navy Yard enjoys elegant quarters. OPPOSITE: Actors from the USS Constitution Museum's living-history program "Tales of the USS Constitution"—left to right, Michele Proude as Anne Hull, Brian Turner as George Sirian, and Rose-Ann San Martino as Mrs. Broaders—pose by the ship's bow. The museum is located adjacent to "Old Ironsides" in the Charleston Navy Yard. The ship, built in 1797 at Boston's Hartt's Shipyard, is the oldest com-misioned vessel in the U.S. Navy—and, in fact, the oldest in the world. It was undefeated in battles against pirates off North Africa's Barbary Coast, and again against the British in the War of 1812. On Independence Day each year and on special occasions, it still takes a tour of the harbor, firing its cannons in celebration.

The ornate 1854 Five Cents Savings Bank Building (above) in Charlestown was originally a Masonic hall. Charlestown—now a northern suburb—was founded in 1629, a year before Boston. The entire port town was razed by the British in the Revolutionary War. Several fine yachts still berth at the Boston Waterfront Marina (right) at Long Wharf. The New England Aquarium (overleaf) is located at Central Wharf. The aquarium features the world's largest observation tank—a 187,000-gallon, four-story structure in which some of the more than two thousand species swim. Feeding time—five times a day—is not just a surface operation; divers take morsels right to the animals. There's a floating marine mammal pavilion, and the aquarium sponsors whale-watching cruises offshore.

Nathaniel Hawthorne once worked as a customs inspector at the 1847 Custom House Block (left) off Atlantic Avenue on Long Wharf. At the time, Long Wharf extended far out into the harbor, and it was lined with ships and warehouses. An elevated interstate highway (above) effectively cut off easy access to the waterfront area from the rest of the city. The familiar archway in the Rowe's Wharf complex of buildings is part of the Boston Harbor Hotel. In the 1990s, the city began massive—and even more disruptive—construction of a project designed to bury the interstate highway, open the waterfront, demolish the overhead freeway, and create a delightful pedestrian mall.

The elaborate, renovated, granite-block Grain and Flour Exchange Building (right) on Milk Street was designed by Shepley, Rutan, and Coolidge—disciples of H. H. Richardson and his Romanesque style—and constructed in the early 1890s. The Custom House (opposite), built between 1837 and 1847, was Boston's most-photographed landmark well into the twentieth century. It was situated on State Street, between the busy waterfront and the banks and government offices inland. Boston had a 125-foot height limit, but the Federal Government was exempt, so when the seventeen-story tower was added to the old Custom House in 1911, Boston got a surprise skyscraper. OVERLEAF: The city's financial district today is a bustling, cosmopolitan area whose skyscrapers are somewhat modest by modern standards.

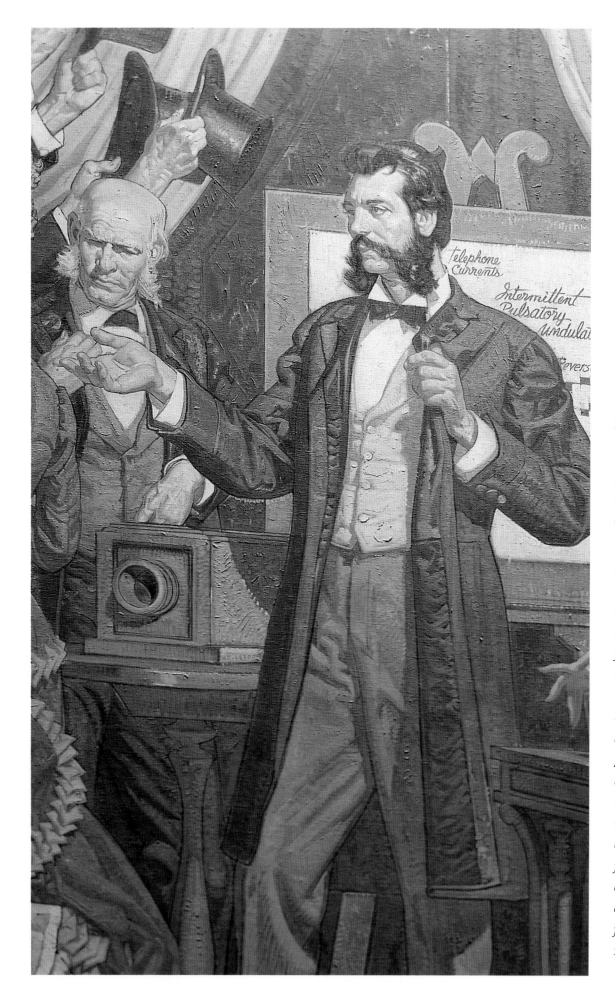

OPPOSITE: *The NYNEX telephone company maintains Alexander Graham Bell's workshop off the lobby of the New England Telephone Building. In that garret room—which was meticulously moved to this location when the original building was demolished in the destruction of Scollay Square—Bell first transmitted the human voice by telephone. Also in the NYNEX headquarters building is Dean Cornwell's mural,* Telephone Men and Women at Work. *Bell (left), shown demonstrating his invention at Lyceum Hall in Salem in 1877, is one of the 197 lifesize figures depicted in the mural. This was the first news event ever reported, appropriately, by telephone. The mural, depicting the industry's pioneers, heroic men and women, and everyday employees— from early male operators to billing clerks and linemen— forms a complete, 160-foot-long oval.*

On the brig Beaver II (right), a faithful replica of one of the ships forcibly boarded and unceremoniously unloaded during the Boston Tea Party of December 16, 1773, the "party" is re-enacted for tourists. The old New England Fish Exchange Building (opposite) is now the headquarters of "Massport"—the Massachusetts Port Authority. OVERLEAF: At the Computer Museum, across the Congress Street Bridge in South Boston, visitors can venture inside the Walk-Through Computer™ 2000. It's a working personal computer the size of a two-story house, surrounded by multimedia boards, connected to a CD-ROM drive, and "networked"—at fifty times scale. Visitors can control the entire computer by delivering instructions through a seven-foot-square Pentium processor; lights then represent the flow of information that follows.

Outside Boston's Computer Museum and Children's Museum, display art turns functional at an ice-cream stand inside a giant Hood's Milk Bottle (above). In the Children's Museum (right), exhibits include a hands-on depiction of aquatic life "Under the Dock." The fifteen-hundred-square-foot exhibit—one of a series with environmental themes—simulates the underwater landscape of Fort Point Channel, complete with a fourteen-foot fiberglass lobster, a dockside puppet theater, barnacle-encrusted dock pilings, and tanks of live lobsters and sea squirts. OVERLEAF: Restaurants and fish markets like the Barking Crab line the Fan Pier across the Northern Bridge. They offer a stellar view of downtown Boston.

Boston's small but vibrant Chinatown (above) is watched over by fu dogs—and, occasionally, inquisitive children. "Chinatown" is a misnomer, for the neighborhood is bursting with people of Laotian, Vietnamese, and Cambodian—as well as Chinese—descent. The 1928 Savoy Theatre (right), with its ornate Spanish baroque façade, was originally a vaudeville house and later the city's opera house. When the Washington Street neighborhood declined precipitously, the building was almost lost. But in the late 1990s it was saved, and extensive renovations began. Two adjacent historic theaters—the Paramount and the Modern—were also rescued. Just inside the Public Garden stands a monument to philanthropist (and patriot Nathan Hale's nephew) Edward Everett Hale, whom a plaque describes as a "man of letters, preacher of the gospel, prophet of peace."

A lush, idyllic lagoon (left), lined with weeping willows and other exotic trees, is the centerpiece of the Public Garden, which was created in 1837 as a decorative, flowery, Victorian-style park specifically designed for langorous meandering. The garden was created over what had been Back Bay salt marshes. Swan boats (above), which have glided atop the lagoon since 1877, were created by Robert Paget, an English immigrant and Boston shipbuilder. He was inspired by Richard Wagner's opera Lohengrin, in which a boat drawn by swans carries the hero across a river. The pedal-powered boats carry tourists past real (and often hungry) ducks, geese, and, occasionally, swans.

Visitors may rent boats for a sail at the Charles River Esplanade (above). At the end of most days, marina workers motor out to corral pleasure sailors whose crafts are becalmed, or who are so taken by the peaceful surroundings that they neglect to head for port. The Esplanade began as a humble walkway, but in 1931 James J. Storrow provided funds to build a waterfront park. Outdoor concerts and ballet at the park's Hatch Shell attract large crowds. Ironically, a multilane commuter highway that slashed through in 1951, robbing the Esplanade of green space, is named for Storrow. OPPOSITE: Back Bay homes face away from the Charles. That's because the river at that point, before it was dammed and purified, was a mudflat and unofficial sewer— hardly desirable waterfront property. So builders oriented their homes in the area to Beacon Street.

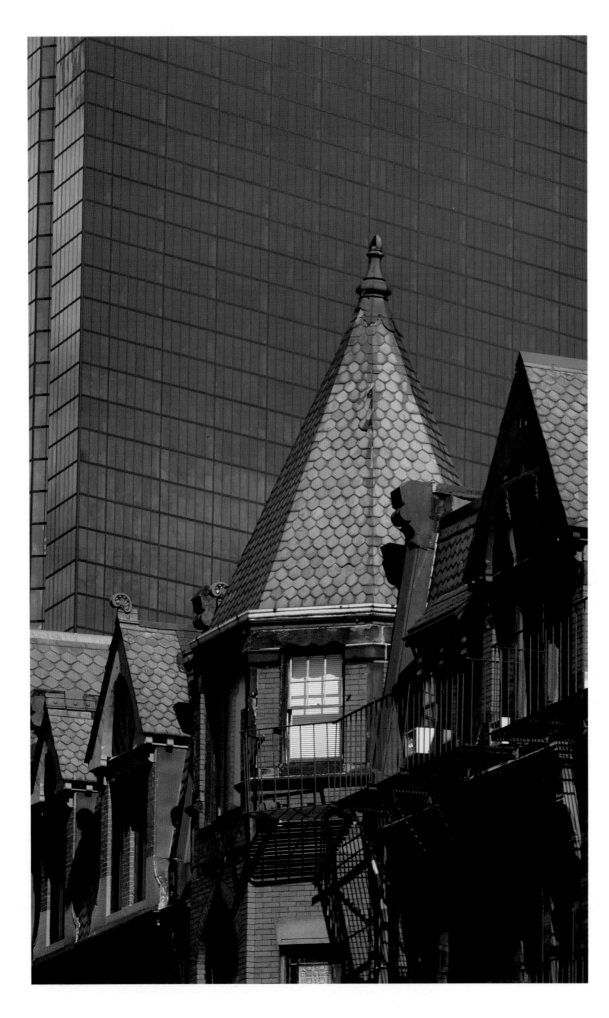

Now the city's most recognizable landmark is the John Hancock Tower (opposite), an I. M. Pei creation that took the name of a 1947 building of the same name. (The latter still stands, its weather beacon steadfastly alerting Bostonians according to an old refrain: "Clear blue, clear view;/ Flashing blue, clouds due;/ Steady red, rain ahead;/ Flashing red, snow ahead.") The newer, sixty-two-story glass rhomboid contains 10,344 "lights" of glass, each weighing five hundred pounds. Every one was replaced after several panes shattered and fell. Hancock security guards used to stand watch on the old building's roof, alert for telltale signs that another pane was in danger of exploding. The rooftops of fashionable Newbury Street row houses (left) form a dramatic contrast to the looming tower.

Copley Square is a lively and architecturally fascinating place. A Gothic-style church (right) with a contradiction as its name—the New Old South Church—rose on Boylston Street in 1874–75 after the congregation moved from its Washington Street meetinghouse (where plans for the Boston Tea Party were hatched). OVERLEAF: In the 1870s, Henry Hobson Richardson executed the incredible Trinity Church, which sits on 4,500 wooden pilings submerged into Back Bay's spongy soil. More than two thousand pilings support the eleven-million-pound lantern tower alone. The interior of the great Episcopal church, executed by John La Farge and other artists, is equally majestic. Not all of Copley Square's statuary is ponderous; there's a place for the whimsical (above) as well.

SAINT·LUKE

M·MAGDALEN

SAINT·JOHN

The inscription on the lion's pedestal reads:

WINCHESTER - 1862 - CEDAR MOUNTAIN -
ANTIETAM - CHANCELLORSVILLE -
GETTYSBURG - RESACA - ATLANTA -
THE MARCH TO THE SEA - SAVANNAH -
SHERMAN'S CAROLINA CAMPAIGN -

Phillips Brooks, who composed the Christmas carol "O Little Town of Bethlehem," was rector when the massive new Trinity Church (opposite) was completed. Across Copley Square, stone lions (above) inside the entrance hall of McKim, Mead & White's 1895 Boston Public Library main building salute Massachusetts regiments in the Civil War. Outside, wrought-iron lanterns (overleaf) illuminate the entrance. Sculptor Daniel Chester French designed the building's massive bronze doors. Inside, in the room where books were once delivered to browsers via a tiny train, are murals depicting *The Quest of the Holy Grail* and *The Triumph of Time.* Into the building's parapets, the names of 519 important persons in the history of civilization have been carved (the artisans mistakenly repeated four of the names). The library's courtyard contains a fountain, a reflecting pool, and plenty of places to sit and read.

Commonwealth Avenue, or simply "Comm Av," as Bostonians refer to it, is a wide, restful boulevard of brownstones and other elegant townhouses (right and overleaf). The avenue's mall, extending westward from the Public Garden, continues the "Emerald Necklace," the interconnected Boston park system designed by the "father of landscape architecture," Frederick Law Olmsted. The Comm Av mall makes a picturesque front yard for the avenue's fortunate residents.
OPPOSITE: *On Newbury Street, "Boston's Madison Avenue" in the Back Bay, creative director James David Bennette, architectural muralist Joshua Winer, and master painter Jack Keledjian created a gigantic, fanciful mural around the corner from the DuBarry French restaurant. It depicts some of history's most famous personages, including, under the left umbrella, Henry Wadsworth Longfellow, and under the right, Babe Ruth.*

One of several monuments on the Comm Av mall, at the Charlesgate entryway to the Back Bay, is a heroic statue of Leif Erickson, "son of Erik, who sailed from Iceland and landed on this continent, A.D. 1000." The avenue's thirty-two acres were designed in French boulevard style by Arthur Gilman in 1856, and the mall was a favorite Victorian place to promenade. Arthur Vinal's 1885 Engine and Hose House No. 33 (opposite) on Boylston Street was extensively renovated in the early 1970s. It adjoins Boston's Institute of Contemporary Art. Boylston Street, which cuts the Back Bay in two, is an important shopping and dining address and home to the Prudential Center, a mixed-use highrise that, like the Hancock Building, features a popular observation deck.

Designed in the 1870s on the French model of sweeping boulevards, gardens, and a tight grid plan, Boston's Back Bay is full of turrets and other fascinating architectural details (above). Only after a massive landfill of pestiferous tidal flats could grand Back Bay buildings be constructed.

The 1906 "Mother Church" of Christian Science (right) is a part of Christian Science World Headquarters on Massachusetts Avenue. The complex began with a small chapel in the 1890s. Charles E. Brigham and Solon S. Beman's colossal basilica seats five thousand people and features the largest pipe organ in the Western Hemisphere. In the 1970s, I. M. Pei and Partners added a headquarters building, Sunday School building, and reflecting pool.

On streets like Warren Street (right), the eclectic South End is full of what Bostonians call "bowfronts"—buildings whose bay windows reach all the way from ground to roof level. Most were constructed in the 1850s, when the Back Bay to the north was still mainly a bog, separated from the South End by a series of railroad tracks. Originally a pleasant Victorian neighborhood built on landfill around The Neck—a narrow strip of land that, amazingly, was once the only land approach to Boston—the South End deteriorated badly before enjoying a revitalization in the 1990s. Even today it is a neighborhood for the upwardly mobile, where students and young couples get a start. Though Tremont Street is a major traffic and business artery, it has blocks of handsome residences (opposite) as well.

Lively Tremont Street in the South End is full of flower shops (above), antique stores (opposite), and an amazing variety of ethnic and other specialty restaurants.

Boston's South End, off the beaten track for tourists, offers Victorian bowfronts, unusual shops, and cozy parks. It is a perfect place for people watchers,

as the neighborhood is the city's most diverse racially, economically, and religiously. The area's many parks often feature small festivals, art and craft fairs, and other

gatherings. Many of the neighborhood's townhouses have been subdivided and subdivided again, increasing the population density. Come September,

the streets are jammed with students, their parents, and their cars, as the South End is a favorite enclave for students of the area's many universities.

Boston's old trolleys still run along Huntington Avenue in the South End (above). South Boston—not to be confused with the South End—is full of warehouses (right), produce and fish companies, restaurants, and museums. Fenway Park (overleaf) is one of baseball's most historic ballparks. It seats only 34,000 fans, most of whom get a close-up view of the action. The park's "Green Monster," just 315 feet from home plate, tempts right-handed batters and bedevils left-handed pitchers. Yet two of the hometown Red Sox's greatest batters— Ted Williams and Carl Yazstremski— hit left-handed. So did one of baseball's greatest sluggers, Babe Ruth, but he was a pitcher in Boston, and the Sox traded him to the Yankees before his career blossomed.

Flamboyant Boston hostess Isabella Stewart Gardner unveiled her private art collection at the Fenway Court (left) in her new Venetian-style villa in 1903. When she died in 1924, her will stipulated that all of the artwork remain displayed exactly as it was at that time, or else it would all be sold and the proceeds turned over to Harvard University. To date, the Isabella Stewart Gardner Museum remains open in Boston's Fenway section. Nearly two thousand objects are on display in Veronese, Dutch, Titian, and other rooms. OPPOSITE: Boston's Museum of Fine Arts, one of the nation's finest art repositories, moved to the Fenway in 1909. Hometown artist John Singleton Copley is one of several American masters whose work is featured here. Its collection of Asiatic art is the largest under one roof in the world.

RIGHT: A sculpture in front of Boston University's Ralph Adams Cram Chapel honors Martin Luther King Jr., who earned his doctorate degree at the nation's fifth-largest private university. OPPOSITE: Tall reeds, two attractive bridges, community "victory garden" plots, three war memorials, and several sports fields can be found in the marshy Back Bay Fens. This area was a stinking repository of sewage runoff until landscape architect Frederick Law Olmstead was brought in to transform it into "public pleasure gardens." Sculling is a passion all along the Charles River (overleaf). Not far from this John W. Weeks footbridge are several boathouses where Harvard and other university students practice almost year-round for spirited competitions.

The striking tower of Dunster House dormitory (right) is one of many landmarks on the Harvard University campus. None is more symbolic of scholarship than Widener Library on Harvard Yard (opposite and overleaf), completed by African-American architect Julian Francis Abele, who had also designed the Widener family mansion in Newport, R.I. The library honors family patriarch Harry Elkins Widener, who died aboard the Titanic. The library houses the second-largest collection of books in America (behind only the Library of Congress), including a Gutenberg Bible and a Shakespeare folio. Harvard boasts two art museums and a huge museum of cultural and natural history.

Boston's Museum of Science, which straddles the Charles River dam in the city's old West End, features more than four hundred exhibits but is perhaps best known for its twenty-foot-high model of Tyrannosaurus Rex *(above)*. Massachusetts Institute of Technology was relocated from a downtown campus (where it was known as Boston Tech) to landfill atop a marsh across the Charles River at the start of the twentieth century. MIT graduate William Welles Bosworth designed the university's signature Maclaurin Building *(right)*. MIT's campus is just as bustling as Harvard's upriver, though more prosaic, practical, and less picturesque, architecturally. Its profusion of laboratories earned it the nickname "The Factory."

The genius of landscape architect Frederick Law Olmsted was evident at Chicago's World's Columbian Exposition, New York's Central Park, Boston's Emerald Necklace, and in many other greenswards nationwide. Olmsted, who had no formal design training, moved to Fairsted (left), his estate and studio in the Boston suburb of Brookline, in 1883 at the height of his career. There, nearly two hundred different varieties of trees, shrubs, and ground covers were planted. At Olmsted's Arnold Arboretum (above), more than fifteen thousand shrubs, vines, and trees—including this stunning array of lilacs—grow on 265 acres. Many were arranged by genus and family by scientist Charles Sprague Sargent.

Sedate Brookline
offers a surprising
attraction in the
carriage house of the
old Larz and Isabel
Anderson estate. It's
a compact museum
of transportation, fea-
turing many of Larz
Anderson's collection
of thirty-three auto-
mobiles. Thanks to
additional donations
such as a 1909
Locomobile (above),
known as "the best-
built car in America,"
the collection now
tops two hundred
vintage cars. Larz
Anderson was a U.S.
ambassador to Japan;
Isabel wrote wildly
popular children's
stories. RIGHT:
On Beals Street in
Brookline stands the
home where John F.
Kennedy was born
on May 29, 1917.
Four of Joseph and
Rose Kennedy's nine
children were born
in the modest house
in the years when
the elder Kennedy
began to amass a
fortune as a financier.

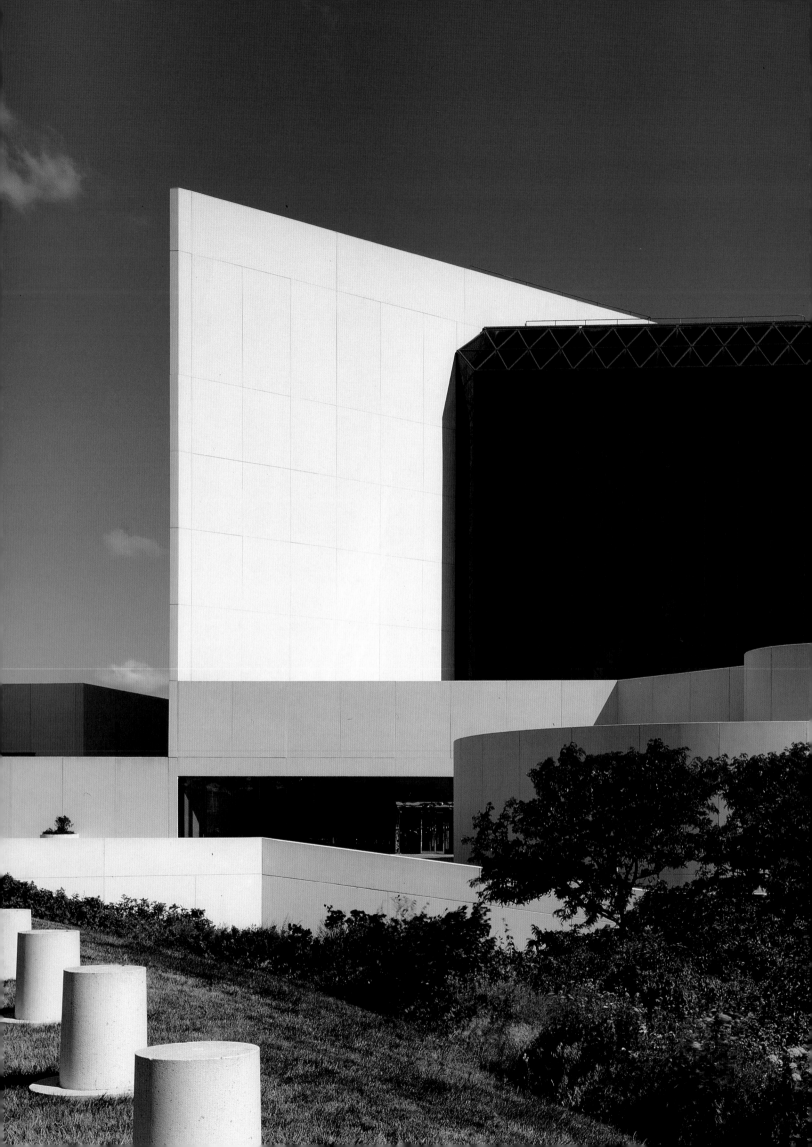

Architect I. M. Pei designed the New Museum at the John F. Kennedy Library (left) overlooking Boston Harbor. The museum recreates the world of the Kennedy presidency, including a replica of the Oval Office (above) and several examples of the decorating touches of First Lady Jacqueline Bouvier Kennedy. There are also twenty video presentations, including the first televised presidential debate with Richard Nixon. President Kennedy's desk and the coconut shell on which he carved a distress call after his PT boat was sunk in the Pacific during World War II are among the items displayed. His beloved sailboat, Victura, is kept on the plaza outside, and the point is planted with some of the family's favorite flora associated with their Hyannis Port compound on Cape Cod.

A Boston visit often includes a journey to Revolutionary War sites in nearby Lexington and Concord. The "Line of the Minute Men, April 19, 1775" is remembered in an 1892 statue on the Lexington Common (right), where a Captain Parker is supposed to have said, "Stand your guard. Don't fire until fired upon. But if they mean to have a war, let it begin here." At the Old North Bridge in Concord (opposite), Minute Men fired the shot heard 'round the world that inflicted the Revolution's first British casualties. Tranquillity is the mood at Walden Pond (overleaf) near Concord, where swimming and fishing have replaced transcendentalist Henry David Thoreau's contemplation in a one-room cabin on the shoreline, and conservationists have successfully kept commercial development at bay.

A lighthouse (above) is but one allurement on the serene island of Nantucket—a favorite nearby relaxation destination. More than one-third of Nantucket's land is preserved in its natural state in perpetuity. Nantucket has a rigid architectural code that keeps the island's cabins relatively uniform in design. Cape Cod Peninsula is closer, livelier, and more crowded. But distinctive Cape Cod cottages (opposite) off the main roads provide ample opportunities for escape from the bustle. Visitors are advised to avoid Friday afternoon journeys to the Cape (or Sunday afternoon returns) in summertime, however, when it seems as if half of Boston is endeavoring to cross the Sagamore Bridge.

Index

Lexington-area residents dress the part of soldiers to bring colonial history alive for visiting school groups.

A small monument and graveyard to Americans who fell at Lexington can be found elsewhere on the green.